How To Be A
Relationships

IT'S TIME TO GROW UP

Master What It Means To Be A
Stable and Loving Partner

ERIC POPE

Table of Contents

Chapter 1:

Understanding Yourself

Today we're going to talk about a topic that hopefully helps you become more aware of who you are as a person. And why do you exist right here and right now on this Earth. Because if we don't know who we are, if we don't understand ourselves, then how can we expect to other stand and relate to others? And why we even matter?

How many of you think that you can describe yourself accurately? If someone were to ask you exactly who you are, what would you say? Most of us would say we are Teachers, doctors, lawyers, etc. We would associate our lives with our profession.

But is that really what we are really all about?

Today I want to ask you not what you do, and not let your career define you, but rather what makes you feel truly alive and connected with the world? What is it about your profession that made you want to dedicated your life and time to it? Is there something about the job that makes you want to get up everyday and show up for the work, or is it merely to collect the paycheck at the end of the month?

I believe that that there is something in each and everyone of us that makes us who we are, and keeps us truly alive and full. For those that dedicate their lives to be Teachers, maybe they see themselves as an educator, a role model, a person who is in charge of helping a kid grow up, a nurturer, a parental figure. For Doctors, maybe they see themselves as healers, as someone who feels passionate about bringing life to someone. Whatever it may be, there is more to them than their careers.

For me, I see myself as a future caregiver, and to enrich the lives of my family members. That is something that I feel is one of my purpose in life. That I was born, not to provide for my family monetary per se, but to provide the care and support for them in their old age. That is one of my primary objectives. Otherwise, I see and understand myself as a person who loves to share knowledge with others, as I am doing right now. I love to help others in some way of form, either to inspire them, to lift their spirits, or to just be there for them when they need a crying shoulder. I love to help others fulfill their greatest potential, and it fills my heart with joy knowing that someone has benefitted from my advice. From what I have to say. And that what i have to say actually does hold some merit, some substance, and it is helping the lives of someone out there.. to help them make better decisions, and to help the, realise that life is truly wonderful. That is who i am.

Whenever I try to do something outside of that sphere, when what I do does not help someone in some way or another, I feel a sense of dread. I feel that what I do becomes misaligned with my calling, and I drag my feet each day to get those tasks done. That is something that I have realized about myself. And it might be happening to you too.

If u do not know exactly who you are and why you are here on this Earth, i highly encourage you to take the time to go on a self-discovery journey, however long it may take, to figure that out. Only when you know exactly who you are, can you start doing the work that aligns with ur purpose and calling. I don't meant this is in a religious way, but i believe that each and every one of us are here for a reason, whether it may to serve others, to help your fellow human beings, or to share your talents with the world, we should all be doing something with our lives that is at least close to that, if not exactly that.

So I challenge each and everyone of you to take this seriously because I believe you will be much happier for it. Start aligning your work with your purpose and you will find that life is truly worth living.

Chapter 2:

How To Succeed In Life

"You can't climb the ladder of success with your hands in your pocket."

Every day that you're living, make a habit of making the most out of it. Make a habit of winning today. Don't dwell on the past, don't worry about the future. You just have to make sure that you're winning today. Move a little forward every day; take a little step every day. And when you're giving your fruitful efforts, you're making sure you're achieving your day, then you start to built confidence within yourselves. Confidence is when you close your eyes at night and see a vision, a dream, a goal, and you believe that you're going to achieve it. When you're doing things, when you're productive the whole day, then that long journey will become short in a matter of time.

Make yourself a power list for each day. Take a sheet of paper, write Monday on top of it and then write five critical, productive, actionable tasks that you're going to do that day. After doing the task, cross it off. Repeat the process every day of every week of every month till you get closer to achieving your goals, your dreams. It doesn't matter if you're doing the same tasks every day or how minor or major they are; what matters is that it's creating momentum in things that you've believed you couldn't do. And as soon as the momentum gets completed, you start to believe that you can do something. You eventually stop writing your tasks

9

down because now they've become your new habits. You need a reminder for them. You don't need to cross them off because you're going to do them. The power list helps you win the day. You're stepping out of your comfort zone, doing something that looks uncomfortable for starters, but while doing this, even for a year, you will see yourself standing five years from where you're standing today.

Decide, commit, act, succeed, repeat. If you want to be an inspiration to others, a motivator to others, impact others somehow, you have to self-evaluate certain perceptions and think that'll help you change the way you see yourself and the world. Perseverance, hard-working, and consistency would be the keywords if one were to achieve success in life. You just have to keep yourself focused on your ultimate goal. You will fall a hundred times. There's always stumbling on the way. But if you have the skill, the power, the instinct to get yourself back up every time you fall, and to dig yourself out of the whole, then no one can stop you. You have to control the situation, Don't ever let the situation control you. You're living life exactly as it should be. If you don't like what you're living in, then consider changing the aspects. The person you are right now versus the person you want to be in the future, there's only a fine line between the two that you have to come face-to-face with.

Your creativity is at most powerful the moment you open your eyes and start your day. That's when you get the opportunity to steer your emotions and thoughts in the direction that you want them to go, not the other way around. Every failure is a step closer to success. We won't succeed on the first try, and we will never have it perfect by trying it only once. But we can master the art of not giving up. We dare to take risks. If we never fail, we never get the chance of getting something we never had. We can never taste the fruits of success without falling. The difference between successful people and those who aren't successful is the point of giving up.

Success isn't about perfection. Instead, it's about getting out of bed each day, clearing the dust off you, and thinking like a champion, a winner, going on about your day, being productive, and making the most out of it. Remember that the mind controls your body; your body doesn't hold your mind. You have to make yourself mentally tough to overcome the fears and challenges that come in the way of your goals. As soon as you get up in the morning, start thinking about anything or anyone that you're grateful for. Your focus should be on making yourself feel good and confident enough to get yourself through the day.

The negative emotions that we experience, like pain or rejection, or frustration, cannot always make our lives miserable. Instead, we can consider them as our most incredible friends that'll drive us to success. When people succeed, they tend to party. When they fail, they tend to ponder. And the pondering helps us get the most victories in our lives. You're here, into another day, still breathing fine, that means you got another chance, to better yourself, to be able to right your wrongs. Everyone has a more significant potential than the roles they put themselves in.

Trust yourself always. Trust your instinct—no matter what or how anyone thinks. You're perfectly capable of doing things your way. Even if they go wrong, you always learn something from them. Don't ever listen to the naysayers. You've probably heard a million times that you can't do this and you can't do that, or it's never even been done before. So what? So what if no one has ever done it before. That's more of the reason for you to do it since you'll become the first person to do it. Change that 'You can't' into 'Yes, I definitely can.' Muhammad Ali, one of the greatest boxers to walk on the face of this planet, was once asked, 'how many sit-ups do you do?' to which he replied, 'I don't count my sit-ups. I only start counting when it starts hurting. When I feel pain, that's when I start counting because that's when it really counts.' So we get a wonderful lesson to work tirelessly and shamelessly if we were to achieve our dreams. Dr. Arnold Schwarzenegger beautifully summed up life's successes in 6 simple rules; Trust yourself, Break some rules, Don't be afraid to fail, Ignore the naysayers, Work like hell, And give something back.

Chapter 3:

The Only Obstacle Is Yourself

Ever wondered why you feel low all the time?

Why it seems like everyone is better than you?

Why everyone excels at something that you wished you were good at too?

I am sure you have wondered about at least one of these at one or another instance in your life.

These questions remain unanswered no matter how hard you try. Until you realize that the only answer that fits the puzzle is that, it is because of you.

All these barriers and limitations are placed upon you not because you are stupid or incapable.

It is merely because you have limiting beliefs about yourself that stop you from achieving your fullest potential.

It is because you are not trying hard enough to make yourself stand apart from everyone else in the world.

If you lag at school, study hard.

If your lag at your job, socialize more.

If you are obese, break a sweat to lose all that fat.

If you lack some technical skill, learn till you beat the very best in that field.

Don't blame others for your failures.
Everyone else starts off with the same resources and expertise as you.
If others can succeed, Why can't you?
Who is stopping you from flying high in victory?
If no one else tells you, let me do the honors; it's you.

You are the biggest cause of everything that is happening in your life right now.
Nothing is good or bad unless you do or don't do something to generate that result.

Make a promise to yourself today that you will achieve something great by the end of this week.
Envision the big picture and start watching yourself get drawn into that picture.

Take baby steps. take a big leap of faith.
Move one foot forward over the other no matter how big or small.
Once you get past the fear of being stuck where you currently are,
life will start opening great doors to your every step forward.

Sometimes we may take a step back.
Sometimes life throws us durians instead of lemons.

As long as you dust yourself off and move again you are never going to lose.

Don't idealize someone if you are not ready to idealize yourself.
To envision yourself charting your own path, in your own unique pair of shoes.

If for whatever reason you don't achieve that something someday, don't beat yourself up for it.
Maybe those shoes weren't the right fit for you.
Try another pair of shoes, and walk down a new path with confidence.

This could be a blessing in disguise for you.
A lesson for you to strive towards something new.
Something better. Something that no one has ever dreamed of or done before.

If along the way some someone comes and tells you to stop, and you stop to hear them say that to you, it wasn't their fault, but yours. Because you were idle enough to be distracted by others to compromise that dream.

Don't lift your head until you have achieved something today. Don't say a word to anyone about your goals.

Spend more and more time to figure out your life. Promise yourself that no one else matters in your life till you have achieved everything and you are left with nothing more to achieve.

I remember the time my father told me to be a better man than him. The time when I fell off my bicycle for the first time. He came to me and said, 'Don't give up now, as you will fall every day, but when you rise you will achieve bigger and better things than you could ever wish'.

My father gave me his hand when I needed it the most and he still does. But when he is gone and there is no one free enough or caring enough left to see me go through all that struggle, then I will be the closest figure to my father to back me up and give me the courage to get up and start again till I succeed in riding the bike of life.

You and I are capable of riding the high tide. Either we ride it all the way to the shore or we drown to never get back up again. It's up to us now what we want to do. It's you who decides what you were and what you can be!

You will regret yourself the most when you finally come to realize that it was 'You' who brought you down. So don't waste yourself and make a vow today, a vow to be the best you can be and the rest will be history.

Chapter 4:

Reach Peak Motivation

Remember the time when you wanted a sign, a person, a comment, an event, just anything that could maybe make you realize once again that everything is happening for real and that you actually have a presence? Remember the feeling?

I am sure we all had those times. And we often still have and maybe have some more to come. But the question is a big mystery that everyone goes through with a rough answer alongside it.

We all have a vague idea somewhere in our heads. We all have some idea somewhere wandering within us but we cease t find it with all our efforts going in vain. There is this struggle with the world that we keep fighting and then there is this quest that we always seem to be on, where we keep looking for answers.

Let me give you some tips for that. You are looking for motivation within yourself because you think the world can't do one for you. It is true to most extent, but the world is not your servant. Nature still gives you things to be proud of and be inspired from. But we keep neglecting the signs of nature.

Situations often present themselves as if we are not meant to be where we are right now. It may be true. But then the world starts to push you down, you will always find reasons at the bottom from where you would want to take a new step forward!

You will always find new ways to become motivated and inspired. Because you need to be dead to become hopeless and motionless, not wanting to do one more thing that could contribute towards a better life.

Till the day you are alive, it's a sin for you to feel hopeless and without purpose.

The fear of failure is always real. But the fear of not being able to feel content and happy once you reach the top is not a reason to not look or stop looking for newer and better things.

Life has endless possibilities and not all have to be bad always. You will get bigger and better chances more than often. But you have to remain motivated enough to avail them for better once they finally present themselves.

You don't have to be bad to fail at something. Even the best of the best fail and they fail more than a regular person. But that doesn't give them a reason to stop rather they get more motivated and energetic to stick to the cause and for what they believe in.

If one thing is important enough and you believe in it enough you will always stay connected to that thing someway or somehow.

But for that, you have to believe in your abilities. That no matter what happens, if you stay committed enough, there is no way in heaven or hell that can keep you away from success and the things that you most want in your life.

Every mountain is within reach if you keep going and keep believing that you are one more step close to the summit.

Chapter 5:

Never Giving Up

Today I'm going to talk about a topic that I feel very inspired to share. In recent times, never giving up has helped me to push through the initial failures that I had experienced when it came to my career which I later found traction in. I hope that the story today will inspire you also do the same.

It Is all too easy for us to give up when the going gets tough. Starting something new is always much easier but sticking through it and grinding through all the problems that you will most certainly face, is the greater challenge on the road to success that many of us are not willing to put ourselves through.

In recent years, I have had many occasions that it was my persistence that actually yielded the fruits of my labour 2-3 years after I had begun the journey. Success was not found immediately.

A few years ago, I began my online career to make money and I found a new business that I was interested in. I invested time and money into it and found some success in the beginning. I gave up all prior aspirations to pursue a traditional career to embark on this journey and I had nothing to lose.

However after 2 years pouring my heart and soul in this venture, I faced a tough reality when something happened to my business and I lost everything. I lost my sole stream of income and I felt absolutely lost, not to mention crushed that all my time had literally gone up in smoke. I started to doubt myself and question why I even bothered embarking on this path in the first place. I really did not know what to do and had no Plan B. I spent the next few months wandering about trying to figure out what's next. At one point I did feel like giving up and going back to finding a regular job despite knowing that that is something I really did not want to do.

After months of exploring, I decided that I would give my first venture another go. I created a new account and began the journey again, from scratch. I faced many obstacles that were not there before and the struggle was terribly real. I felt pressure from myself to make it work because I felt that there was nothing I was really good at. I needed to prove to myself that I wasn't a failure and that fire lit up inside me to be successful at it at all cost.

To put it simply, eventually my persistence did pay off and I managed to build back some of the income stream that I had lost with new strategies that I had employed. What I only realised much later was that it was actually my experience having been in the business for two years prior that helped me navigate this new strategy much quicker. Everything was done at lightning speed despite the obstacles and I was astounded by the pace in which it picked up. It was in that moment that I understood the principle of never giving up. Because if I had, I would have literally flushed away all the time and energy I had invested earlier in the business down the toilet. It was my attitude of never giving up, and learning from my mistakes that got me through the second time around.

Another story that I want to share about never giving up is something much simpler, and it had to Do with something that happened around the house. In a random event, somehow my door got jammed by an appliance around the house. And no matter how hard I tried to push it simply wouldn't budge. After cracking my head for hours, together with my parents, we still couldn't figure out how to get the door to open no matter how many things we tried. At one point my dad decided that the only way was to break down the door. However the persistence in me didn't want to give up. I found a strategy that could possibly work, involving a knife, and long story short I managed to get the door to open with a great deal of strength. In that moment I felt like the king of the world. Never giving up and persisting felt like the greatest feeling on Earth. And it got me fired up to want to apply this same persistence to all aspects of my life.

It was with these joint experiences along with many others that gave me the conviction that solidified the principle that I have been hearing from gurus every single day about never giving up. That only when you had given up have you truly failed. And I believe every single one of those words today.

So I challenge each and everyone of you today to try this out for yourself. To go back to something you have decided that you had called quits on and to give it one more try. Use your expertise, use your experience, learn from your mistakes of what went wrong before, modify the new plan, and try again. You might be surprised at the outcome. Never ever give up because it's never really over until you have decided to quit.

Chapter 6:

Living in the Moment

Today we're going to talk about a topic that will help those of you struggling with fears and anxieties about your past and even about your future. And I hope that at the end of this video, you may be able to live a life that is truly more present and full.

So what is living in the moment all about and why should we even bother?

You see, for many of us, since we're young, we've been told to plan for our future. And we always feel like we're never enough until we achieve the next best grade in class, get into a great university, get a high paying career, and then retire comfortably. We always look at our life as an endless competition, and that we believe that there will always be more time to have fun and enjoy life later when we have worked our asses off and clawed our way to success. Measures that are either set by our parents, society, or our peers. And this constant desire to look ahead, while is a good motivator if done in moderation and not obsessively, can lead us to always being unhappy in our current present moment.

Because we are always chasing something bigger, the goal post keeps moving farther and farther away every time we reach one. And the reality is that we will never ever be happy with ourselves at any point if that becomes our motto. We try to look so far ahead all the time that we miss the beautiful sights along the way. We miss the whole point of our goals which is not to want the end goal so eagerly, but to actually enjoy the process, enjoy the journey, and enjoy each step along the way. The struggles, the sadness, the accomplishments, the joy. When we stop checking out the flowers around us, and when we stop looking around the beautiful sights, the destination becomes less amazing.

Reminding ourselves to live in the present helps us keep things in perspective that yes, even though our ultimate dream is to be this and that career wise, or whatever it may be, that we must not forget that life is precious and that each day is a blessing and that we should cherish each living day as if it were your last.

Forget the idea that you might have 30 years to work before you can tell ur self that you can finally relax and retire. Because you never know if you will even have tomorrow. If you are always reminded that life is fragile and that your life isn't always guaranteed, that you become more aware that you need to live in the moment in order to live your best life. Rid yourself of any worries, anxieties, and fears you have about the future because the time will come when it comes. Things will happen for you eventually so long as you do what you need to do each and every day without obsessing over it.

Sometimes our past failures and shortcomings in the workplace can have an adverse effect on how we view the present as well. And this cycle perpetuates itself over and over again and we lose sight of what's really important to us. Our family, our friends, our pets, and we neglect them or neglect to spend enough time with them thinking we have so much time left. But we fail to remember again that life does not always work the way we want it to. And we need to be careful not to fall into that trap that we have complete and total control over our life and how our plans would work out.

In the next video we will talk about how to live in the moment if you have anxieties and fears about things unrelated to work. Whether it be a family issue or a health issue. I want to address that in a separate topic.

Chapter 7:

10 Signs You've Outgrown Your Life

Growth can be hard, but it is necessary sometimes you outgrow your life, and understandably it is the scar you are required to stretch yourself to something you haven't been familiar with. Growth demands you to take risks and leave your comfort behind. Another important aspect is that you should be vulnerable because whenever there is growth, failure is there. Leaving your old life behind is scary, but the alternative to that is even scarier because staying in the same position for a long time can be soul-crushing. Here are ten signs that you have outgrown your life

1. You Can No Longer Relate To The People Around You

When you realize that you are surrounded by people you have nothing to talk about, it's an obvious sign that you have outgrown them. There is also a chance that you stop enjoying the activities you previously participated in and enjoyed with them, plus communication feels like a struggle. You will receive comments from your close circle that you have changed, and you won't exactly be happy with those comments but be prepared. Others telling you that you have changed should be considered a compliment. It simply means you're growing.

2. Everyone Around You Is Changing

Another sign of you outgrowing your life is that everyone around you is changing as well. If your friends and family are making all kinds of changes in their lives and you're sitting alone on some barstool, it's time to take inventory of your life. You have outgrown your old life, so now it's time to set some new goals.

3. You Have A Constant Feeling of Discontent

Constant dissatisfaction when you were previously content with the same circumstances is a huge sign of outgrowing your life. The reason could be your current life doesn't challenge you the way it once did, and when life isn't challenging, it becomes mundane, and depression creeps in. Living in discontentment is not a way to live. You should listen to your inner voice and make some changes.

4. You're Interested In Different Things

Being interested in different activities that you previously found boring and they vastly deviate from what you found interesting that simply means you are outgrowing your current life. You should follow this inclination and engage yourself in new things. It will keep your life fresh and exciting!

5. You Fantasize About Having A Different Life

Constantly dreaming about how you wish your life was a sure sign. If you were obsessed with your life, you wouldn't be consistently envisioning a different one.

Maybe you think about living in a new city, having a new job, having different relationships, and/or new hobbies.

Recognize that you've outgrown your life and make those fantasies a reality!

6. You Have New Goals That Are Vastly Different Than Your Life

Having goals and working toward them is one of the healthiest things you can do for yourself!

BUT if your new goals would change the course of your life, you've likely outgrown your life.

7. You're Bored With Your Life

You might be bored with your job or career. Maybe you're bored with your relationships and the activities you used to love.

If your days feel dull, you're ready to shake your life up!

It's one thing to feel bored here and there but being bored EVERY DAY of your life is an awful way to live and a glaringly huge sign you've outgrown your life!

8. You Feel Like You're Going Through The Motions

This is a BIG sign you've started to outgrow your life.

If you wake up every day with zero enthusiasm and move throughout the day on autopilot, you're ready for huge life changes.

I've had points in my life where I was just getting through the day simply existing. It's a depressing way to live.

Don't accept a mundane life for yourself. Make the changes necessary to get excited about your days!

9. You Start Trying To Fill A Void

Maybe you're doing it with shopping, food, alcohol, sex, etc. This one can be hard to identify because you might just think you lack discipline or control.

Take inventory of the thoughts you have when you're tempted to engage in your addiction. Are you trying to numb feelings of dissatisfaction with your life?

10. Your Vision Board Is 100% Unrelated to Any Part of Your Current Life

This was a HUGE eye-opener for me. When I created my vision board in the New Year, it was different from my life. I have since begun to take steps to make my vision board my reality.

What does your vision board look like? Is it different than your current life? If so, you've likely outgrown your life.

What can you do to start making your vision board a reality?

Chapter 8:

Happy People Reward Themselves

Do you ever wonder if the carrot and stick principle would still work in this world? The answer to this would be yes, the reward and punishment system still works, and you can always leverage it to build good habits. They, in turn, will help you reach your goal faster; that is why it is essential to celebrate your hard work and then afterward reward yourself for the effort you have been putting in. Gretchen Rubin, in her book Better than before, says,

"When we give ourselves treats, we feel energized, cared for, and contented, which boosts our self-command — and self-command helps us maintain our healthy habits."

If you do not get any rewards and treats, you will feel resentful angry, and you feel depleted. Imagine putting in all the hard work and then not getting anything in return. How would that make you feel? Bad, right? That is precisely why rewarding yourself is essential. We are going to outline 2 simple reasons why rewarding yourself is important.

1. Reward makes you feel good and drives you further.

How do you train pets, your dogs, and cats? You teach them with a treat. Just like them, our brain works the same way we can train ourselves to do a lot more work by rewarding ourselves. When you give yourself a treat, you will boost your mood, making you happy. When you give yourself a treat, your brain releases a chemical called dopamine that makes you feel good and happy. Even tho it is important to reward yourself, not all rewards give the same effect, and you should choose wisely so that those treats create positive reinforcement.

2. It works as positive reinforcement.

When a pleasant outcome follows your behavior, you are more likely to repeat the behavior. And this is called positive reinforcement. Connecting your hard work to rewards effectively not only gives you a mental break but also motivates you to want to do more of it. Therefore, use treats as positive reinforcement to build your momentum and grow your habits.

Just like this powerful saying from Tony Robbins:

"People who succeed have momentum. The more they succeed, the more they want to succeed, and the more they find a way to succeed. Similarly, when someone is failing, the tendency is to get on a downward spiral that can even become a self-fulfilling prophecy.

Chapter 9:

7 Ways To Attract Happiness

We have seen a lot of people defining success as to their best of knowledge. While happiness is subjective from person to person, there's a law of attraction that remains constant for everyone in the world. It states that you will indirectly start to attract all the good things in life when you become happier. This is why happy people often have good lives where everything just somehow tends to work for them. Happiness not only feels good but can also make our manifestation attempts twice as effective. We shouldn't measure our happiness from external factors but instead, as cliche as it may sound, we should know that true happiness comes from the inside.

Here are some ways for you to attract happiness:

1. Make a choice to be happy:

When you choose to be as happy as you can in every moment of your life, your subconscious mind will start acknowledging your decision, and it will begin to find ways to bring more joy into your life. When you work towards your decision of being happy, the universe also plays its part and makes sure it attracts more situations in your life that you can be pleased about. The positive vibrations that you will give out will find their way back to you. You don't have to make the decision of being happy right away, as some of you might be going through a tough time. Sit, relax, and take some time to reflect on yourself first and then make a choice whenever you're ready.

2. Define What Happiness Means To You

We have also found ourselves asking this question a million times, "what exactly is happiness?" Some people would attach the idea of happiness with materialistic things such as a big house, expensive cars, branded clothes and shoes, designer bags, the latest technologies, and so forth. While for some, happiness is merely spending time with family and friends, doing the things that they love, and finding inner peace and calm.

3. React Positively under all situations:

We could experience a thousand good things but a million bad ones in our everyday lives. And sometimes, it could be complicated for us to encounter any kind of happiness given the circumstances. Although these circumstances cannot be in our control, how we react to them is always in our hands. As our favorite Professor Dumbledore once said, "Happiness can be found even in the darkest of times if only one remembers to turn on the light." Similarly, we should always try to find that silver lining at the end of the dark tunnel, always seek some positivity in every situation. But we are only humans. Don't try to enforce positivity on yourself if you don't feel like it. It's okay to address all our emotions equally till you be yourself again.

4. Do not procrastinate:

You might find it a bit weird, but procrastination does snatch your happiness away. No matter how much things are going well in your life, you would always find a loophole, a reason to be unhappy and dissatisfy with yourself a well as your life. Procrastination makes you believe that you are not living up to your fullest potential. You will get this nagging feeling that will eventually morph into negative emotions that would nearly eat you. So, try to avoid procrastination as much as possible and start doing the things that actually matter.

5. Stay present:

The key to becoming more focused, more at peace, more effective in manifesting, and eventually, much happier is to just live in the moment. Whatever you're doing in the present, try to be completely aware and focused on it. It will help you avoid all the negative feelings you have conjured up about the past and future. Try to stay present as much as you can; over time, it will become a habit, and you will develop the capability to face it all. This will definitely help you attract more happiness into your life.

6. Do not compare yourself:

As Theodore Rosevelt once said, "Comparison is the thief of joy." Whenever we compare ourselves to others, we tend to become ungrateful and strip ourselves of the ability to appreciate the good and abundance in our lives. We start to magnify the good in other people's lives and the bad that is in our own. We must understand that everyone is going through their own pace, and they all are secretly struggling with one thing or the other.

7. Don't try too hard:

Happiness demands patience. It is better to get into it gradually rather than being overeager. Many people take the law of attraction and being positive a little too far and start obsessing over it. They tend to panic if they get negative thoughts or are unable to attract the things they want. Don't get frustrated if things don't work out your way, and don't give up on the idea of happiness if you feel distressed. Try to prioritize your happiness and give others a reason to be happy too. Make yours as well as other's lives easy.

Conclusion:

Not many people know that, but being happy is actually the foundation towards attracting all your dreams and goals. When you adopt the habit of becoming truly happy every day, everything good will naturally follow you. Over time, happiness can even become your default state. Try your best to follow the guidelines above, and I guarantee that you will start feeling happier immediately.

Chapter 10:

7 Ways To Discover Your Strengths

It is a fact that everybody has at least one skill, one talent, and one gift that is unique to them only. Everyone has their own set of strengths and weaknesses. Helen Keller was blind but her talent of speaking moved the world. Stephen Hawking theorised the genesis by sitting paralyzed in a wheelchair. The barber who does your hair must have a gifted hand for setting YOUR hair at reasonable prices—otherwise you wouldn't be visiting them.

See, the thing is, everyone is a prodigy at one thing or another. It's only waiting to be discovered and harnessed. Keeping that fact in mind...

Here are 7 Ways You can Discover Your Potential Strengths and Change Your Life Forever:

1. Try Doing Things That You Have Never Done

Imagine what would have happened if Elvis Presley never tried singing, if Michael Jordan never tried playing basketball or if Mark Zuckerberg never tried coding. These individuals would have been completely different persons, serving different purposes in life. Even the whole world would've been different today if some specific people didn't try doing some specific things in their lives.

Unfortunately, many of us never get to know what we are truly good at only because we don't choose to do new things. We don't feel the need to try and explore things that we have never done before in our lives. As a result, our gifted talents remain undiscovered and many of us die with it. So while the time is high, do as many different things you can and see what suits you naturally. That is how you can discover your talent and afterwards, it's only a matter of time before you put it to good use and see your life change dramatically.

2. Don't Get Too Comfortable With Your Current State

It is often the case that we cling on to our current state of being and feel absolutely comfortable in doing so. In some cases, people may even embrace the job that they don't like doing only because 'it pays enough'. And honestly, I totally respect their point of view, it's up to people what makes them happy. But if you ask me how one can discover their hidden talents—how one might distinguish oneself—then I'm going to have to say that never get used to doing one particular thing. If one job or activity occupies you so much that you can't even think of something else, then you can never go out to venture about doing new stuff. The key is to get out, or should I say 'break out' from what you are doing right now and move on to the next thing. What is the next thing you might want to try doing before you die? Life is short, you don't want to go on your whole life, never having experienced something out of your comfort bubble.

3. What Is The Easiest Thing You Can Do?

Have you ever found yourself in a place where you did something for the first time and immediately you stood out from the others? If yes, then chances are, that thing might be one of your natural strengths.

If you've seen 'Forrest Gump', you should remember the scene where Forrest plays table-tennis for the first time in a hospital and he's just perfect at the game. "For some reason, ping-pong came very naturally to me, so I started playing it all the time. I played ping-pong even when I didn't have anyone to play ping-pong with.", says Forrest in the movie.

So bottomline, pay attention to it if something comes about being 'too easy' for you. Who knows, you might be the world's best at it.

4. Take Self-Assessment Tests

There are countless, free self-assessment tests that are available online in all different kinds of formats. Just google it and take as many tests you like. Some of these are just plain and general aptitude tests or IQ tests, personality tests etc. while there are others which are more particular and tell you what type of job is suited for you, what kind of skills you might have, what you might be good at, and those kinds of things. These tests are nothing but a number of carefully scripted questions which reveal a certain result based on how you answered each question. A typical quiz wouldn't take more than 30 minutes while there are some short and long quizzes which might take 15 minutes and 45 minutes respectively.

Though the results are not very accurate, it can do a pretty good job at giving you a comprehensive, shallow idea of who you are and what you can be good at.

5. Make Notes On How You Deal With Your Problems

Everyone faces difficult situations and overcomes them in one way or the other. That's just life. You have problems, you deal with them, you move on and repeat.

But trouble comes in all shapes and sizes and with that, you are forced to explore your problem-solving skills—you change your strategies and tactics—and while at it, sometimes you do things that are extraordinary for you, without even realizing it. John Pemberton was trying out a way to solve his headache problem using Coca leaves and Kola nuts, but incidentally he made the world's coke-drink without even knowing about it. Lesson to be learned, see how YOU deal with certain problems and why is it different from the others who are trying to solve the same problem as you.

6. Ask Your Closest Friends and Family

People who spend a lot of time with you, whether it be your friend, family or even a colleague gets to see you closely, how you work, how you behave, how you function overall. They know what kind of a person you are and at one point, they can see through you in a manner that you yourself never can. So, go ahead and talk to them, ask them what THEY think your strongest suit can be—listen to them, try doing what they think you might turn out to be really good at, Who knows?

7. Challenge Yourself

The growth of a human being directly corresponds to the amount of challenge a person faces from time to time. The more a person struggles, the more he or she grows—unlocks newer sets of skills and strengths. This is a lifelong process and there's no limit on how far you can go, how high your talents can accomplish.

Now, one might say, "what if I don't have to struggle too much? What if my life is going easy on me?". For them, I'd say "invite trouble". Because if you are eager to know about your skills and strengths (I assume you are since you're reading this), you must make yourself face difficulties and grow from those experiences. Each challenge you encounter and overcome redefines your total strength.

Final Thoughts

To sum it up, your life is in your hands, under your control. But life is short and you gotta move fast. Stop pursuing what you are not supposed to do and set out to find your natural talents RIGHT NOW. Once you get to know your strengths, you will have met your purpose in life.

Chapter 11:

How To Have The Best Day Everyday

We all have the power to create the kind of day we want to experience every time we go to sleep and wake up the next day.

It is normal to think that we will only have an amazing day when something good happens to us. We believe that good things only happen out of luck, chance, fate, or whatever, but we never think that we can create a good day just by our sheer desire to.

What the best day means to each of us may be different, some prioritise professional accomplishments as their measurement of a great day, some prioritise spending time with as many friends as possibly in a 24 hour period as one that is great. But when we depend on these circumstances, we are never really in full control of our day because bad things can always happen without a rhyme or reason. Our presentation that we have been working months on could suddenly be marred by a technical difficulty, or our friends could cancel on us last minute due to whatever reason.

What we thought would be our best day could turn out to be one filled with disappointments and maybe even loneliness.

I struggle with this all the time. Everytime i had built up the perfect day in my head, something always seem to go wrong somehow and I am left searching for a filler to cover that void. Through the fault of nobody but life getting the way, as it always does, I found out that if I always depended on others to give me the best day, that it rarely ever happens. Occasionally things work out great when I least expect it, but those occurrences are still out of my control.

It is only when we decide for ourselves that we can have the best day regardless of life inserting itself in, that we can truly enjoy every waking moment of our lives. By constantly reminding ourselves that we are grateful to be alive, to live each moment in the present, and to live as though tomorrow might never come, we can truly appreciate the little things in life that we often overlook. We have the best day because we believe that it is.

From the moment that we get out of bed, we appreciate the first breath we take, the first shower that we take, the first meal that we take, and all the little things that make up our wonderful day. Appreciating the fact that we are living with a roof over our heads, that we have clean water to drink, air conditioning to keep us cool, heaters to keep us warm, literally anything and everything around us, there is something to be grateful for.

When we start to notice that our life is truly amazing, we will never have to depend on other things or other people to make us have our best day. That is the kind of control we have over our day if we set it off on the right foot from the get-go.

It was only when I started being grateful for the fact that I am truly blessed with an amazing family, pet, friends, a house, that I realized i didn't need fancy party or fancy things to allow me to have the best day ever. Yes there are moments in life when we feel truly alive, those moments we will cherish and remember, but those moments are also few and far between. If we can take control of the other 364 days of the year, we would truly be the happiest people alive on this earth who are living their best days everyday.

Chapter 12:

9 Tips on How To Have A Strong Relationship

Who doesn't want a strong relationship? Everyone wants to have that high-level understanding with their partner that lasts a lifetime. It is scientifically proven that people who are in healthy relationships have less stress and more happiness.

Healthy relationship not only helps us increase our overall feelings of happiness, but stress-reduction also helps us improve our overall quality of physical and mental health that make every-day life more pleasing to go through. Relationships can be in the form of family, work, friendships, and also romantic ones. Depending on the area that matters the most to you at this very point in your life, you can choose to focus on that specific one until you feel you are ready to focus on the next.

If building powerful relationships is a priority of yours as it is mine, then stay with me till the end of this video because we will be discussing **9 Magical** Tips on How To Have A Strong Relationship with whoever you want. Let's Begin.

Number one

Listen to Each Other

This is the first and probably the most important thing that you might want to take note of. Just think, how many arguments have you had that went in the wrong direction just because no one was willing to simply just listen? In order to understand each other's point of view both parties must be willing to open up their ears instead of their mouths first. You need to have the stamina to listen to their side of the story before airing yours.

If you truly want a healthy relationship then the foundations starts with a good listening ear. To listen not only when the other party have problems in their lives, but also when they have a problem with you. Develop a good sense of compassion and empathy in the process.

Bitter thoughts, grudge-holding, and negativity toward the other person only serve to weaken your relationships, not strengthen them. So try to understand each other, let the other person speak, and then sort things out in the best possible way.

Number two

Give Time For The Relationship To Grow

For any relationship to truly blossom, it is important to spend the necessary quality time together. Whether the relationship is with family members, friends, or lovers, it takes energy and effort nonetheless. Any amount of energy you spend on that person will reap its benefits later. Now, I am not saying to drastically change your life or to go on adventures or expensive dates to make your relationship healthy. All you have to do is simply get yourself free for a day or night once a week and do something different together, like having a date night, playing games, cooking and eating, watching movies or whatever you like, just give your best at that time. Be present with them and don't be distracted checking your phone or replying work messages.

Number three
Give Time To Yourself

Now I needed to talk about this one right after the number two. I think a good relationship should be balanced. In the previous point, I talked about spending quality time in relationships, but I also don't mean that you should give all your energy to them or stop doing things that energizes your soul. Don't sacrifice your own hobbies for the sake of others. I agree that you need to take more initiative in relationships but at the same time you need to take care of your own happiness too. So give time to yourself and spend it doing things that fills your soul with happiness and gratefulness. You will feel recharged and fresh as a result when you engage in your relationships.

Number four
Learn To Appreciate Little Things

This point will touch more on the romantic relationship side of things. If you are in a relationship for quite a while then there is a chance that you might get complacent and too comfortable. You might also gradually forget the little things that make the person special. As a result the other person could potentially feel like you may be taking them for granted. To avoid this, you need to start making it a constant reminder to yourself to appreciate the little things your partner does for you. Say "I love you" to them, give cute little gifts, give them surprises and tell them how much they mean to you. You need to show your partner how much you love them so they never feel taken for granted. So yeah, start doing all this and make your bond strong!!

Number five
Learn To Forgive

It is well said, "relationships require a lot of forgiveness". As I mentioned earlier, bitter thoughts and grudge-holding just hurt your relationship in the long run. So if you want a happy relationship then you should learn to forgive. If there is something on your mind that your partner did and you can't forget then sit and talk to them about it and try to come up with a good solution. If any of you makes any mistake, you should forgive them with a smiling face and tell them that these little mistakes can't lessen your love. Work on yourself, make your heart ready for what you see coming and even what you don't see coming, and let things go in the right direction. You need to make your heart learn to forgive, this is the only key.

Number Six
Don't expect your partner to complete you

You should be confident about whatever you have. If you are looking for a healthy relationship then you should not expect your partner to complete you. Sometimes, we expect things from our partners which we lack and it can put a strain on your relationship. What you could do instead is to constantly work on yourself to the point that you feel you truly and rightfully deserving of every good thing that comes your way. That you feel secure and independent at the same time in the relationship. Loving yourself first goes a long way in maintaining a strong and healthy relationship with others.

Number Seven
Ways Of Showing Love

Different people show and receive love in their own unique ways. Understanding how the other party expresses or receives love is the key to building a strong relationship. Some people do it by caring for you while others express it through physical affection like hugs and kisses. If you don't know that the specific love language is between you and the other party then it might cause problems in the long run. To really ensure the other party feels loved you have to express it in the way that they receive the most strongly. Go find out what they are by asking them and then start giving it right away!

Number eight
Be Flexible

If you want a healthy relationship then you have to learn to be flexible as well. Flexible in the face of any changes that might occur in your relationship. It is a known fact that change is the only constant in life. We may never be prepared but we should do our best to adapt to new situations that we may find ourselves in. It is also therefore unrealistic not to expect our relationships to change as time progresses as well. Learn to adapt and grow in this new stage and you will be all the more happier for it.

Number nine

Make Decisions Jointly

A good and healthy relationship requires listening to each others' desires and concerns. While you may not always love to do the things that the other party wants, you should always try to find a compromise that suits both of your needs. Instead of insisting and making decisions all the time, try making decisions together that both of you will find enjoyable. Be it where to hang out, what to eat for a meal, where to go on a trip together, or even what kinds of products to buy for your home, make sure that the other party's points of view is heard so that they don't end up resenting you over the long run.

So that's it, guys, we are done with our today's topic of 9 Tips on How To Have A Strong Relationship. Now, it's time for you to share your thoughts. What do you think about these tips? Have you already tried them and do they work? And if you know some other tips to make relationships strong then share them in the comment box to help others. If you got value then smash the like button and don't forget to subscribe to our channel as we will be talking about some amazing topics in the future. See you soon!

Chapter 13:

Becoming High Achievers

By becoming high achievers we become high off life, what better feeling is there than aiming for something you thought was unrealistic and then actually hitting that goal.

What better feeling is there than declaring we will do something against the perceived odds and then actually doing it.

To be a high achiever you must be a believer,

You must believe in yourself and believe that dream is possible for you.

It doesn't matter what anyone else thinks , as long as you believe,

To be a high achiever we must hunger to achieve.

To be an action taker.

Moving forward no matter what.

High achievers do not quit.

Keeping that vision in their minds eye until it becomes reality, no matter what.

Your biggest dream is protected by fear , loss and pain.

We must conquer all 3 of these impostors to walk through the door.

Not many do , most are still fighting fear and if they lose the battle, they quit.

Loss and pain are part of life.

Losses are hard on all of us.

Whether we lose possessions, whether we lose friends, whether we lose our jobs, or whether we lose family members.

Losing doesn't mean you have lost.

Losses are may be a tough pill to swallow, but they are essential because we cannot truly succeed until we fail.

We can't have the perfect relationship if we stay in a toxic one, and we can't have the life we desire until we make room by letting go of the old.

The 3 imposters that cause us so much terror are actually the first signs of our success.

So walk through fear in courage , look at loss as an eventual gain, and know that the pain is part of the game and without it you would be weak.

Becoming a high achiever requires a single minded focus on your goal, full commitment and an unnatural amount of persistence and work.

We must define what high achievement means to us individually, set the bar high and accept nothing less.

The achievement should not be money as money is not our currency but a tool.

The real currency is time and your result is the time you get to experience the world's places and products , so the result should always be that.

The holiday home , the fast car and the lifestyle of being healthy and wealthy, those are merely motivations to work towards. Like Carrots on a stick.

High achievement is individual to all of us, it means different things to each of us,

But if we are going to go for it we might as well go all out for the life we want, should we not?

I don't think we beat the odds of 1 in 400 trillion to be born, just to settle for mediocrity, did we?

Being a high achiever is in your DNA , if you can beat the odds , you can beat anything.

It is all about self-belief and confidence, we must have the confidence to take the action required and often the risk.

Risk is difficult for people and it's a difficult tight rope to walk. The line between risk and recklessness is razor thin.

Taking risks feels unnatural, not surprisingly as we all grew up in a health and safety bubble with all advice pointing towards safe and secure ways.

But the reward is often in the risk and sometimes a leap of blind faith is required. This is what stops most of us - the fear of the unknown.

The truth is the path to success is foggy and we can only ever see one step ahead , we have to imagine the result and know it's somewhere down this foggy path and keep moving forward with our new life in mind.

Know that we can make it but be aware that along the path we will be met by fear , loss and pain and the bigger our goal the bigger these monsters will be.

The top achievers financially are fanatical about their work and often work 100+ hours per week.

Some often work day and night until a project is successful.

Being a high achiever requires giving more than what is expected, standing out for the high standard of your work because being known as number 1 in your field will pay you abundantly.

Being an innovator, thinking outside the box for better practices, creating superior products to your competition because quality is more rewarding than quantity.

Maximizing the quality of your products and services to give assurance to your customers that your company is the number 1 choice.

What can we do differently to bring a better result to the table and a better experience for our customers?

We must think about questions like that because change is inevitable and without thinking like that we get left behind, but if we keep asking that, we can successfully ride the wave of change straight to the beach of our desired results.

The route to your success is by making people happy because none of us can do anything alone, we must earn the money and to earn it we must make either our employers or employees and customers happy.

To engage in self-promotion and positive interaction with those around us, we must be polite and positive with everyone, even with our competition.

Because really the only competition is ourselves and that is all we should focus on.

Self-mastery, how can I do better than yesterday?

What can I do different today that will improve my circumstances for tomorrow.

Little changes add up to a big one.

The belief and persistence towards your desired results should be 100%, I will carry on until... is the right attitude.

We must declare to ourselves that we will do this , we don't yet know how but we know that we will.

Because high achievers like yourselves know that to make it you must endure and persist untill you win.

High achievers have an unnatural grit and thick skin , often doing what others won't, putting in the extra hours when others don't.

After you endure loss and conquer pain , the sky is the limit, and high achievers never settle until they are finished.

Chapter 14:

How To Be Your Own Best friend

Why would you want to become your own best friend? There are several benefits to creating your internal support system rather than relying on your partner, friends, or family to be there for you when you're suffering. Having other people's expectations can lead to disappointment, heartbreak, and relationship breakdown if your expectations aren't met. We all have it in us to give ourselves what we need without seeking it externally.

Of course, it's great if you have a strong support network, but you could still benefit from becoming more self-reliant. And what about if you have no one to turn to for help, or if your current support people are unable to be there for you?

Isn't it far better to know how to support yourself in times of need? Here's how to become your own best friend.

1. Be Nice To Yourself

The first step to becoming a friend is to treat yourself like you would treat a friend. That means that you need to stop being self-critical and beating yourself up. Start by acknowledging your good qualities, talents, and abilities and begin to appreciate your unique self.

When you catch yourself thinking up some nasty self-talk, stop and ask, "Would I say this to my best friend?" If not, then reframe your self-talk to be more supportive and caring.

2. Imagine How You Would Support A Friend In The Same Situation

Think about a loved one, a friend, a family member, someone dear to you and imagine that they are in the same situation you are currently facing. Think about how they're struggling, suffering, and feeling stuck with this problem, then consider how to best offer assistance and advice to them.

Craft the words that you would say to your greatest friend and then say them gently to yourself. Allow yourself to feel supported, and give yourself what you need.

3. Honor Your Needs

Following the theme of considering how you would help a dear friend, **you need to start taking your advice and putting your own needs first**. Do you need a day off from work? A long hot bath? An early night? A wild night? Some time to catch up on your reading, cleaning, gardening, creative projects, social life, or self-care?

Whatever you need, allow yourself to **put it at the top of the list rather than the bottom**. Be there for yourself and make it happen.

4. Send Compassion To The Part of You That is Hurting

Being a friend to yourself involves adopting and mastering the art of self-compassion. Compassion isn't forceful or solution-focused. **Compassion is accepting, peaceful, and loving, without the need to control or change anything**.

Imagine a mother holding a child who has bumped his head. Her compassion is a strong force. She simply holds her child with loving, comforting, gentle arms and whispers, "It will be alright, my love." The child trusts his mother's words just as you learn to trust your own words when speaking to yourself.

Imagine yourself as both the child and the mother simultaneously. Offer compassion at the same time as you open up to receive it.

Use these techniques to become your own best friend and start *being there* **for yourself!**

Chapter 15:

Friendship The Key To Happiness

Today we're going to talk about the power of friendship and why i believe everyone needs to have at least 1 or 2 close friends in their lives to make life actually meaningful and worth living.

You see, for many years while i was working hard towards my goals, i spent almost all of my time on my business and little to zero time on building Long lasting relationships. And this one sided approach to success left me with a hole that weakened me emotionally, but also physically as well.

In this very myopic view of what I felt success should be and what I felt i needed to do at that point, I prioritised my career first over everything else, neglecting my own personal health, family, and friends. Whenever I was invited for a meal or an outing I always declined, viewing that it was a waste of time. That it was taking time away from my work that i should be focusing on. And as I declined more and more of these offers from friends, the invite also became less and less frequent as they saw me as someone who was either too busy, or just didn't bother to want to take this friendship to the next level.

For a while I was actually happy, that i remember telling myself that yes I dont have plans for the week and that i can focus on my work wholeheartedly. But what i failed to realise was that I was prioritise making money over everything else. And that i was losing the connection with other humans. I started to become more withdrawn, more introverted, and I was losing that spark that i once had when conversing with friends. I wasn't experiencing life enough to have any meaningful moments that I could look back on and say that wow those were great times.

It all became one giant blur and 3 years later, it felt truly pointless. I found myself lonely and without someone I could talk to. I even neglected my best friend to the point that we drifted so far apart that she found other people to confide into. This left me with a sinking feeling that I had failed to prioritise The people around me.

And from that point on I knew i needed to change. I knew i needed to put myself out there once again and shift my priorities to the things that truly mattered. Friends that could ask you out for a quick meal so that you could hash out some of your grievances in life, friends that you can share your happiness as well as your sadness, friends that could provide some meaning to the days you were living, and even more simply, friends that you can count on when all else fails.

You see the business that I spent 3 years building collapsed on me. And I found myself with nothing to show for it. No experiences worth highlighting. Only regrets that I had failed to put others before my selfish needs.

It was a hard climb back to establishing the friendships I once had. People had already started viewing me as a flaker and a no-show that it was now up to me to prove to them that I was open and available to be called a reliable friend once again. Some efforts on my part did not go as I had planned but I kept trying to make new connections, joining new groups, making tennis friends, starting up conversations with new people and asking if they could invite me along to an outing. And these little seeds started to show fruition. I soon found myself getting asked out for meals and games, and life started to feel a little bit better again.

After the initial struggle, the floodgates starting opening and I found myself busy with true life again, connecting with other people on a deep personal and emotional level. And i felt that that was what life was really all about. Friends that you can see yourself hanging out 40 years down the road when you are old and nobody wants you anymore.

I plan to keep sowing these seeds for as long as life allows me and I challenge each and everyone of you to do the same. Businesses and careers may not last, but hopefully the friends that you have made will.

Chapter 16:

How To Have Proper Time Management

Managing time is one of the hardest things to do; our everyday routine revolves around time management. But what does it mean? Some people fail to understand the true meaning of time management. Time management can be defined as planning and controlling how much time to spend on specific activities. When a person knows how to manage his time, he faces less stress and efficiently completes more work in less time.

Everyone now wants to manage their time, the world is moving fast, so must we, but how to do that? The answer is relatively easy. You need to set your goals correctly. Setting your goals correctly would help you save time and so your brain wouldn't be messed up. The SMART method is the best method, where s stands for specific, M stands for measurable, A stands for attainable, R stands for relevant, and T stands for timely. If you set your goals by using the SMART method, you are bound to manage your time.

Now sometimes we all have so much work to do that we forget which one is more important, what you should do is to sit back for a minute, take out your to-do list and see which of your daily task is both important as well as urgent than that task should be your priority and you should do these tasks right away. Some tasks are important but not urgent, you can decide when to do these, but some are neither critical nor urgent you can leave them later to do. Prioritizing your tasks properly helps you manage time.

We all say that this generation is moving fast, but we also know that laziness is in the air. Being lazy is what messes up our routine. "Time is money" we all have heard this but hardly pay attention to this; wasting our time on one task is like ruining our whole plan for the day. You need to set a time limit for every task, depending on its difficulty level. When you have been assigned something to do, estimate the time it would take you to complete that task and set a limit. If you think you don't have enough time to complete the task, then seeking help from someone is not a bad option. But if you don't check the time, you may end up with incomplete work that will cause you a few problems.

Although work is essential, "All work and no play makes Jack a dull boy," this means that when a person is constantly working and burdens himself with the workload, he finds it hard to concentrate because his brain is all fried up. When you have a busy and packed schedule that includes many tasks, try to take small breaks between these tasks. Working constantly will make it hard for you to focus on your next task. You should take a break in the middle of these tasks, try grabbing a brief nap, or you can do something that will freshen up your brain like meditation, jogging, etc.

An organized person feels less messed up; for example, even if your wardrobe is messed up, you feel uncomfortable because this nagging sensation at the back of your head tells you that your closet needs to be organized. Similarly, try managing your calendar for more long-term time management. Try writing on a calendar about appointments, meetings, deadlines, so you don't forget what to do next. If there is something you need to do, then set a few days for that specific task. This method will help you remember more of your task and your plans.

Although time management is hard, it is not impossible. You just need to prioritise, take small breaks and sort out everything and you would be good to go.

Chapter 17:

6 Concerning Effects of Mood On Your Life

By definition, mood is the predominant state of our mind which clouds over all the other emotions and judgements. Our mood represents the surface-level condition of our emotional self.

Mood is very versatile and sensitive. Subtle changes in our surroundings or even changes in our thoughts directly affect mood. And consequently, our mood, being the leader of our mental state, affects us, as a whole—even impacting our life directly.

Take notes of these following points so that you can overpower your mood and take complete control of your life.

Here Are 6 Ways How Changes In Your Mood Can Impact Your Life:

1. Mood On Your Judgement and Decision-Making

Humans are the most rational beings—fitted with the most advanced neural organ, the brain. Scientists say that our brain is capable of making one thousand trillion logical operations per second and yet still, we humans are never surprised to make the stupidest of judgements in real life.

Well, along with such an enormous 'Logical reasoning' capacity, our brains also come with an emotional center and that is where mood comes in to crash all logic. Most of the decisions we make are emotional, not logical. Since our emotions are steered by mood, it is no surprise that we often make irrational decisions out of emotional impulses.

But again, there are also some instances where mood-dictated decisions reap better outcomes compared to a logical decision. That's just life.

2. Mood Affects Your Mental Health

While our mood is a holistic reflection of our mental state caused by various external and internal factors, it is also a fact that our mood can be the outcome of some harboring mental illness. Both high degree of euphoria and depression can be an indication of mood disorder—just on two opposite ends of the spectrum.

There is no specific cause behind it except that it is a culmination of prolonged mood irregularities. And mood irregularities may come from anywhere i.e. worrying, quarrelling, drug abuse, period/puberty, hormonal changes etc. If such mood irregularity persists untreated, it may deteriorate your overall mental health and result in more serious conditions. So, consider monitoring your mood changes often.

3. Correlation Between Mood and Physical Well-Being
We have heard the proverb that goes, "A healthy body is a healthy mind". Basically, our body and mind function together. So, if your body is in a

healthy state, your mind will reflect it by functioning properly as well. If on the other hand your body is not in a healthy state, due to lack of proper nutrition, sleep, and exercise, then your mind will become weak as well. Yes, according to research, having a persistent bad mood can lead to chronic stress which gradually creates hormonal imbalance in your body and thus, diseases like diabetes, hypertension, stroke etc. may arise in your body. Negative moods can also make you go age faster than usual. So having a cheerful mood not only keeps you happy but also fuels your body and keeps you young. Aim to keep your body in tip top condition to nourish the mind as well.

4. Effect Of Your Mood On Others

This is obvious, right? You wouldn't smile back at your significant other after you have lost your wallet, spilled hot coffee all over yourself and missed the only bus to your job interview.

Your mood overshadows how you behave with others. The only way to break out of this would be to meditate and achieve control over your emotional volatility—believe that whatever happened, happened for a reason. Your sully mood doesn't warrant being hostile with others. Instead, talk to people who want the best of you. Express your griefs.

5. Mood As A Catalyst In Your Productivity

Tech giants like Google, Apple, Microsoft all have certain 'play areas' for the employees to go and play different games. It is there to remove mental stress of the employees because mood is an essential factor in determining your productivity at work-place. According to experts, people with a negative mood are 10% less productive in their work than those who are in a positive mood. This correlation between mood and productivity is an important thing to be concerned about.

6. Mood Change Your Perspective

Everyone has their own point of view. Perspectives of people vary from individual to individual and similarly, it varies depending on the mood of an individual. On a bad day, even your favorite Starbucks drink would feel tasteless. It doesn't mean that they made a bad drink—it means that you're not in the mood of enjoying its taste. So, how you perceive things and people is greatly affected by your mindset. Pro-tip: Don't throw judgement over someone or something carrying a bad mood. You'll regret it later and think "I totally misread this".

Final Thoughts

Our mood has plenty of implications on our life. Though our mood is an external representation of our overall mental state, it has its effect on very miniscule aspects of our life to large and macroscopic levels. In the long run, our mood alone can be held responsible for what we have done our whole life—the choices we've made. Though it is really difficult to control our mood, we can always try. Meditating may be one of the possible ways to have our mood on the noose. Because no matter what happens, you wouldn't want your whole life to be an outcome of your emotional impulses would you?

Chapter 18:

5 Ways Quitting Something Can Bring You Joy

Do you ever wonder if you will ever be truly happy in your life? Do you wonder if happiness is just a hoax and success is an illusion? Do you feel like they don't exist? I know a friend who felt like this a little while ago. At the time, she was making a six-figure income, was working for her dream company (Apple), and had a flexible work schedule. Despite all this, she was miserable. She would have never been able to quit my job if not for the practice she got from quitting little things.

Of all the things that she tried, quitting these seven little things made her the happiest.

1. Quit Reading the News

News headlines are usually about happenings around the world. Most times, they are negative. Negative headlines make for better stories than positive headlines. Would you read a headline that says 'Electric Chair Makes a Comeback' or a headline that says 'Legislation debate in Tennessee'? See what I mean.

Journalists have to write stories that interest us. I can't blame them for that. Changing the time that I caught up on the news helped me be more positive during the day. Start reading inspirational posts first thing in the morning instead of news. You can still catch the news later, around 11 am instead of at 6 am.

2. Quit Hunching Your Shoulders

This boosted my confidence levels.

We hunch our shoulders and take up as little space as possible when we feel nervous and not too comfortable. This is body language 101.

Keeping a posture, opening up your shoulders will make you feel more confident during the day. But, I must admit it will make you more tired than usual. It will take you at least a total of 45 days before you start doing this effortlessly.

3. Quit Keeping a Corporate Face at Work

We are all trained not to show real feelings at work. Having a corporate face is good for corporate, not for you. Smiling all day, even when you are upset, will lift your mood. It will make you feel better sooner. Studies have shown that smiling makes you happy.

4. Quit Writing Huge Goals

It is better to write and work towards achievable goals before starting to write our stretch goals. Stretch goals are great to push ourselves. But, we all need achievable goals to boost confidence and to have successes that we can build momentum on. This can be hard for you if you are an overachiever.

5. Quit Eating Fries and Eat Oranges Instead

Fries are comfort food for a lot of people. But eating them saps energy.

Eat oranges instead of fries every time you feel down and feel the need for comfort food. This not only boosts your energy but will also help you lose some pounds if you want to. Plus, this will give you energy and clarity of mind.

Chapter 19:
How Not To Waste Your 25,000 Mornings As An Adult.

Adulthood is the time of our lives when we need to get serious about everything. We have to take care of every single thing from time to our mornings. Early morning is the time of the day when freshness consumes us—known as the best time to work. Why waste such precious time? Having a good morning automatically means having a good day too. When a mind is fresh, it works. And wasting 25,000 mornings of your adulthood would be truly foolish. Those 3571 weeks would go to waste as there was no essential work done.

To make sure that you don't waste your morning is to be sure that you have mornings. Waking up late just automatically means that half of your day has gone to waste. So, wake up early. Those early hours have some courage to work in them. And who wants to waste such an opportunity to prove themselves. Not only will it be beneficial for your professional life, but it will also be beneficial for your health. Get a decent night's sleep, and you will see the changes that come along with them.

After you open your eyes in the morning, immediately sit up. Going back to sleep is always a more intriguing option. But we need to know that our priority is to wake up. And when you are sleeping, make sure that nothing disturbs it. Phone on silent—the tv's off and lights out. Make sure you are as comfortable as possible so you won't wake up the following day grumpy. Disturbance in sleep may cause the disappearance of it. There is a chance that you can't sleep again. That is not what we want. So, we take things beforehand.

An easy way to wake up in the morning is to have some encouragement ready for you. Either it's gym or work. It will make you wake up in the morning early to jump-start whatever you have planned. Then the mornings will be a lot more efficient for you and much more enjoyable. The first thing that we tend to do right after waking up is to check our phones. We waste 20 minutes or more just lying there doing nothing much of a task. Let's get one thing clear. It's not worth it. Wake up in the morning, get a cup of coffee, and start your day without any technology, naturally.

Once you fall into a habit, you will fall into a routine. Your life will change for the good, and you will look towards the brighter side of life. Mornings are a precious time, and 25,000 of our adulthood is the most important morning of our life. So, make sure that you make every morning out of those 25,000 mornings count. It won't be easy, but it will be worth it!

Chapter 20:

How Getting Out of Your Comfort Zone Could Be The Best Thing Ever

A comfort zone is best described as the place where you feel comfortable and your abilities are not being tested, or a place where you don't have to try anything new or different. We have all heard the advice of getting out of our comfort zone. Its sure sounds like an easy phrase, but any advice is easier to give than to take. While it is true that the ability to take risks by stepping outside your comfort zone is the primary way by which we grow, it's also true that we are often afraid to take that first step. Embracing new experiences can bloom your life and could even change the direction of your career. Comfort zones are not really about comfort; and they are about fear. So, break the chains and step out; you will enjoy the process of taking risks and growing. Here are some ways to get out of your comfort zone to experience a better life.

1. Become Aware Of What's Outside The Comfort Zone

You believe so many things are worth doing, but the thought of disappointment and failure always holds you back. Identify the things that you are afraid of doing and assess the discomforts associated with them. Start working on them slowly and gradually. You will see how much progress you will make and how much you will grow following that. Once your discomforts no longer scare you, you will see how confident you will become in trying new things.

2. Have A Clear Sight About What You Have To Overcome

There would be many situations that get you anxious and uncomfortable. Please make a list of all of them and go deeper. The primary emotion associated with all of our negative thoughts that we try to overcome is fear. Are you afraid of public speaking because you are insecure about your voice? Do you get nervous around people and avoid talking to them for fear of being ignored? Be specific in your areas of discomfort, and then work on your insecurities to get more confident.

3. Get Comfortable With Discomfort

Expand your comfort zone to get out of it. Make it your goal to stop running away from the discomforts. If you can't make eye contact while talking, try locking it a bit more rather than immediately looking out. If you stay long enough and practice it, it will start to become less uncomfortable.

4. See Failure As A Teacher

Many of us are so scared of failures that we would prioritize doing absolutely nothing other than taking a shot at our dreams and goals. We have to treat our failures as a teacher. We learn more from failures than we do from successes. Take that experience that has caused you to fail and evaluate how you can take that lesson your next time so that the chance of success increases. Many of the world's famous people, and even billionaires and millionaires, failed the thousandth time before succeeding.

5. Take Baby Steps

Don't try to achieve everything at once. If you jump outside your comfort zone, the chances are that you will become overwhelmed and jump right back in. Always start by taking small steps, overcome the fear of little things first. It's the small steps along the journey that ensures our extraordinary destination. If you are afraid of public speaking, start by speaking to a smaller group of people or even your family and friends. This will help you built self-confidence, and you will be ready to talk on public platforms in no time.

6. Hang out with risk-takers:

If you want to become better at something, start hanging out with people who already took the risk, who already are doing the things you planned to do. Start emulating them. No one can give you the best insight into the situations than those who already have experienced it. Almost inevitably, their influence will start affecting your behavior, and you too will get a clear mind about things.

7. Be Honest With Yourself

Stop making excuses for the things that you are too afraid to do. You might be tricking your brain into thinking that maybe you don't have enough time to do your tasks. But in reality, you are scared of giving it a chance and risking failure. Don't make excuses but instead, be honest. You will be in a better place to confront what is truly bothering you, and this will increase your chance of moving forward.

8. Identify New Opportunities

Staying in your comfort zone is like sitting in a closed room or wearing blinders. You will convince yourself that you already dislike the things you didn't even try yet and only care about the already part of your life. But you have to put your walls down, not thickens them, and take risks. You will be amazed at how many opportunities you will be exposed to when you finally let yourself out.

Conclusion

It will seem scary at first to get out of your comfort zone, but it will be the best experience of your life. Don't jump right out of it; slowly push yourself past your comfort zone. You will eventually feel more and more comfortable about the new stuff you were too afraid to try.

Chapter 21:

Happy People Consciously Nurture A Growth Mindset

"Without continual growth and progress, such words as improvement, achievement, and success have no meaning." – Benjamin Franklin

Learning is perceived and generally acknowledged by those of us who have gone through primary and university tutoring. We were routinely encircled by people who energized and upheld our developments. Groundbreaking thoughts and change were anticipated from us; the sky was the limit!! However, shouldn't something be said about once we got into the work environment? For some, we subsided into the everyday daily practice, getting it done, uninformed of the cost that our agreeable, monotonous, continuous tasks appeared to have on our own and expert development.

Do you hear employees saying, "I don't get how this venture's development works" or "I'm awful at giving introductions. If it's not too much trouble, let another person do it." If this is the case, reconsideration of your group's growth mindset might be in order. They are working under a "fixed mentality." According to an examination concentrate via Carol Dweck of Stanford University, a fixed attitude happens when individuals accept fixed qualities that can't change. These individuals archive abilities instead of attempting to foster them. On the other hand, a development attitude accepts that knowledge can develop with time and experience. When individuals accept they can add to their learning, they understand exertion affects their prosperity.

You can attempt to battle a fixed attitude and energize a sound growth mindset by rehearsing the following:

Recognize fixed mindset patterns

To begin with, would you say you are ready to precisely recognize and uncover the negative quirks coming about because of a fixed mentality? Normal practices of these individuals incorporate the individuals who keep away from challenges, surrender effectively, consider there to be as achieving nothing, overlook and keep away from negative criticism, need heading in their objectives, and carry on when feeling undermined by other people who make progress. These are normal signs that employees are battling to see their part in supporting the new turn of events.

Energize feedback over praise

Commendation feels better. We like to feel approved in our qualities and are content to let it be the point at which we get acclaim over achieved work—employees to request input despite the result. There are consistent approaches to improve and create. Lead your group to request tips and innovative manners by which they can move toward new situations.

Pinpoint skills and limitations

Take time out from the ordinary daily schedule to pinpoint your workers' qualities and shortcomings will give an unmistakable beginning stage to an initiative in realizing where holes exist. Have workers independently take strength evaluations and meet with them to go over outcomes. Some may feel compromised and cautious while going over shortcomings, yet having a direct discussion on the finding will prompt better anticipation and recuperating.

Chapter 22:

<u>Get in the Water (Stop wasting time)</u>

Stop wasting time.

If you have something to do, then do it. It is literally that simple. Nobody likes something hanging over their head, it is stressful and pressurising and the longer you leave it, the more of a challenge it is going to be. Just get it done.

It's like getting into cold water. You can start by dipping your big toe in, then walking away and reconsidering, before putting all five of them in, maybe if you are feeling frisky you'll put in your whole foot. It is such a waste. You know you are going to get in the water eventually so you might as well dive in. Otherwise, you will spend 80% of your time drawing out an adjustment that could literally take a few seconds. What is the point? Just dive in and get it over with. Does it take a bigger first-off effort, yes. But it saves you so much time and energy afterwards. After the initial shock and a few seconds of feeling like your skin is trying to shrivel up, you are fine.

If we can do it with cold water then we can do it with that email, project or book. You can dive right into all that research you need to do. Yes, it seems overwhelming, and that first leap is going to be full of questions and discomfort. Mid-air you will probably be asking what you got yourself into but the great thing is that you can't stop mid-air. There's no turning around and floating on the air until you reach solid ground again. You are committed now.

The powerful thing is that 90% percent of your problem is inertia. It is that first step. It's sitting down, firing up your laptop and starting to work. It is getting past the idea that you have so much work to do and just focussing on what you can do right now. But when it comes down it you must realise that there is no work around for that. You cannot not do that first step. Even if it is just a passion you know that passion is going to keep burning you up on the inside until you allow it to burst out. There's no getting past the cold water, there is only getting into it. So you might as well jump. If you are trying to write a book, then sit down and just start typing. Even if you are not even typing words, just sit down for 25 minutes and type away at your keyboard. Then, while you are typing you will realise that you are sitting down and pressing the keys anyways so they may as well say something that make sense. I don't care if what you type is cliché because at this point we are not worried about quality. I don't care how good your form is in your butterfly stroke if you are not even in the water. You just need to get started so that you are moving. And once you are moving you can maximise on your momentum.

Chapter 23:

Putting Exercise First

In this topic we're going to talk about why you should consider putting exercise first above all else in your daily routine and the benefits that it can bring to your health and all other aspects of your life.

Many of us don't usually prioritise work as the most essential part of our day. We have work, family, kids, money, and a whole host of problems to worry about that exercise usually comes in dead last on the list of things to do. What we fail to realise is that exercise is the one thing that we might need most to keep us fit and healthy to take on the challenges that life throws at us each and every day.

I'm sure you all know the benefits of exercise. Doing it regularly can bring lots of benefits to your metabolism, alertness, energy, BMI, muscle mass, and so on. But what does it really mean?

Have you ever wondered why you are always feeling tired all the time? Or why you feel like you haven't really woken up yet when you're already sitting in front of your desk at the office?

You see, it is the time of your exercise that matters a lot too. A lot of successful CEOs and entrepreneurs actually make exercise the first thing they do when they wake up from bed. The reason is simple, it gets the body moving which in turns starts the engine that drives you out of lethargy and into an active physical state. As you move on a treadmill or do yoga early in the morning, your heart starts pumping faster which drives more blood into other areas of your body to wake you up.

And this sets you up for success because you are no longer in a state of slumber and sluggishness. Exercising first thing in the morning also has the added benefit of checking it off your list early so that you do not wait for the lazy bug to tell you not to enter the gym.

Sure getting up earlier to exercise might also be a struggle in of itself, but you do not necessarily have to travel to a gym far away to get your daily exercise. Simply stepping out of the house for a quick run or finding an empty space in your house where you will not be disturbed and begin a yoga routine that you can find on YouTube will also suffice. As long as you get the body moving and in a state of flow, you would have already won the day.

Putting exercise first above all else in your day also gives you a sense of accomplishment that you have taken the action to improve your health consistently. Losing excess body fat will also increase your energy levels and help you get through the challenges of your work day with greater ease.

If you find that exercising first thing in the morning is just impossible to do for some reason, make it a point to schedule it sometime before midday, preferably during your lunch break. Leaving exercise to the night will only trigger more excuses from your brain not to go as your will power gets depleted more and more throughout the day. From experience, unless I have booked a class that i can't back out of in the evening, more often than not I will find many more excuses not to go than if I had scheduled exercise early in the day.

If there is a sport that you particularly like, I also urge you to schedule more games with friends or family throughout the week as you are more likely to show up for them seeing that you already favour the sport over other exercises. In my case I love tennis and would almost never miss a session that I have scheduled. Gym and yoga on the other hand, I am more inclined to give it a miss if given the opportunity.

So for those of you who want to operate in a higher state of mind, body, and spirit, I challenge you to make exercise your number one priority and put it at the top of your list of things to do for the day. You will find your mind will be clearer and you will know exactly what you need to do for the day as you flow with the exercise. Feel free to play your favourite music playlist as you workout as well.

Chapter 24:

The Power of Community

The topic that we are going to discuss today is something that I feel has resonated with me one a more personal level recently. And it is one that I have largely neglected in the past.

As i have mentioned before in other videos, that as an entrepreneur of sorts, my job required me to work independently, mostly from home. And while it may sound nice to others, or even yourself, where you think it is a privilege to work from home, many a times it is actually not all that fun because there is no sense of community or interaction with others. And the job becomes quite lonesome.

I'm sure many of you who have experienced lockdowns and Work from home situations, that it may seem fun for a week, but after that you realize that actually it isn't all that it is cracked out to be. And you actually do wanna get dressed, get out of the house, and go somewhere to do your work rather than stay in your PJs all day and waste your time away.

But if you dig deeper, you will realize that what you actually miss is the interaction with your co-workers, to just walk over to their desk to ask them something, or simply to just start a conversation because maybe you're bored, or to have lunch together instead of cooking your own instant noodles at home.

As social creatures, we crave that human interaction. And we crave belonging in a community and being a part of something bigger than ourselves.

When we are in lockdown, we lose that personal touch that we have with others, and we start to feel restless, we feel that something is missing but we can't put our finger on it. It is not the actual work at the job that we look forward to, but rather the people, the colleagues that make working fun and enjoyable.

The same goes for any sports of workout. You will realize that when you gym alone, you are less likely to show up because there is no one there to push you to make you do one more rep. There is no community to keep you going back to stick to your goals. For those of you who do yoga, i am sure the experience is very different when you practice an hour of yoga at home versus in a yoga studio with 30 other people, even if you don't know any of them. There is still a sense that you are a part of a greater unit, a class that works out together, a group of like-minded individuals who really want the same thing and share the same interests. You feel compelled to go back because the community is there to make the exercise fun. That after a tiring workout you look to the people beside and around you and you see the same expressions on their faces. That they had shared an activity with you and feel the same things. Isn't that what life is really about? To be a part of something rather than going about it like a lone wolf?

So for those of you who feel like something is amiss in the activity that you once loved, be it a sports or a job, or an activity that you have no choice to do but never felt happy doing it, i challenge you to find a like-minded community who share the same beliefs and interests. You can easily look for such groups on meet-up apps. You might find that the missing puzzle is indeed other individuals that share your likes. And when you work around them or with them, you will feel a much greater sense of joy and happiness that you never thought you could feel.

Chapter 25:

4 Ways Geniuses Come Up with Great Ideas

Following are thumbnail descriptions of strategies common to the thinking styles of creative geniuses in science, art, and industry throughout history.

1. Geniuses Look at Problems in Many Different Ways

Genius often comes from finding a new perspective that no one else has taken. Leonardo da Vinci believed that to gain knowledge about the form of problems, you begin by learning how to restructure them in many different ways. He felt the first way he looked at a problem was too biased toward his usual way of seeing things. He would restructure his problem by looking at it from one perspective and move to another view and still another. With each move, his understanding would deepen, and he would begin to understand the essence of the problem. Einstein's theory of relativity is, in essence, a description of the interaction between different perspectives. Freud's analytical methods were designed to find details that did not fit with traditional perspectives to find a completely new point of view.

In order to creatively solve a problem, the thinker must abandon the initial approach that stems from past experience and re-conceptualize the problem. By not settling with one perspective, geniuses do not merely solve existing problems, like inventing an environmentally friendly fuel. They identify new ones. It does not take a genius to analyze dreams; it required Freud to ask in the first place what meaning dreams carry from our psyche.

2. Geniuses Make Their Thoughts Visible

The explosion of creativity in the Renaissance was intimately tied to the recording and conveying of a vast knowledge in a parallel language, a language of drawings, graphs, and diagrams — as, for instance, in the renowned diagrams of DaVinci and Galileo. Galileo revolutionized science by making his thought visible with charts, maps, and drawings, while his contemporaries used conventional mathematical and verbal approaches.

Once geniuses obtain a certain minimal verbal facility, they seem to develop a skill in visual and spatial abilities, which gives them the flexibility to display information in different ways. When Einstein had thought through a problem, he always found it necessary to formulate his subject in as many different ways as possible, including diagrammatically. He had a very visual mind. He thought in terms of visual and spatial forms rather than thinking along purely mathematical or verbal lines of reasoning. In fact, he believed that words and numbers, as they are written or spoken, did not play a significant role in his thinking process.

3. Geniuses Produce

A distinguishing characteristic of genius is immense productivity. Thomas Edison held 1,093 patents, still the record. He guaranteed productivity by giving himself and his assistants' idea quotas. His own personal quota was one minor invention every ten days and a major innovation every six months. Bach wrote a cantata every week, even when he was sick or exhausted. Mozart produced more than six hundred pieces of music. Einstein is best known for his paper on relativity, but he published 248 other papers. T. S. Elliot's numerous drafts of "The Waste Land" constitute a jumble of good and bad passages that eventually was turned into a masterpiece. In a study of 2,036 scientists throughout history, Dean Kean Simonton of the University of California, Davis found that the most respected produced great works and more "bad" ones. Out of their massive quantity of work came quality. Geniuses produce. Period.

4. Geniuses Make Novel Combinations

Dean Keith Simonton, in his 1989 book Scientific Genius suggests that geniuses are geniuses because they form more novel combinations than the merely talented. His theory has etymology behind it: cogito — "I think — originally connoted "shake together": intelligent the root of "intelligence" means to "select among." This is a clear early intuition about the utility of permitting ideas and thoughts to randomly combine with each other and the utility of selecting from the many the few to retain. Like the highly playful child with a pailful of Legos, a genius constantly combines and recombines ideas, images, and thoughts into different combinations in their conscious and subconscious minds. Consider Einstein's equation, $E=mc^2$. Einstein did not invent the concepts of energy, mass, or speed of light. Instead, by combining these concepts in a novel way, he could look at the same world as everyone else and see something different. The laws of heredity on which the modern science of genetics is based are the results of Gregor Mendel, who combined mathematics and biology to create new science.

Chapter 26:

Don't Overthink Things

Analysis Paralysis, how many of you have heard of this term before? When a decision is placed before us, many of us try to weigh the pros and cons, over and over again, day and night, and never seem to be able to come up with an answer, not even one week later.

I have been guilty of doing such a thing many times in my life, in fact many in the past month alone. What I've come to realize is that there is never going to be a right decision, but that things always work out in the end as long as it is not a rash decision.

Giving careful thought to any big decision is definitely justified. From buying a car, to a house, to moving to another state or country for work, these are big life-changing decisions that could set the course for our professional and financial future for years to come. In these instances, it is okay to take as much time as we need to settle on the right calculated choice for us. Sometimes in these situations, we may not know the right answer as well but we take a leap of faith and hope for the best and that is the only thing we can do. And that is perfectly okay.

But if we translate the time and effort we take in those big projects into daily decisions such as where to go, what to eat, or who to call, we will find ourselves in a terrible predicament multiple times a day. If we overthink the simple things, life just becomes so much more complicated. We end up over-taxing our brain to the point where it does not have much juice left to do other things that are truly important.

The goal is to keep things simple by either limiting your choices or by simply going with your gut. Instead of weighing every single pro and con before making a decision, just go. The amount of time we waste calculating could be better spent into energy for other resources.

I have found that i rarely ever make a right choice even after debating hours on end whether I should go somewhere. Because i would always wonder what if i had gone to the other place instead. The human mind is very funny thing. We always seem to think the grass could be greener on the other side, and so we are never contented with what we have in front of us right here right now.

The next time you are faced with a non-life changing decision, simply flip a coin and just go with the one that the coin has chosen for you. Don't look back and flip the coin the other way unless it is truly what your heart wants. We will never be truly happy with every single choice we make. We can only make the most of it.

Chapter 27:

Why You're Demotivated By A Values Conflict

Every human being, in fact, every organism in this universe is different from even the same member of their species. Every one of us has different traits, likes, dislikes, colors, smells, interests so it's natural to have a difference of opinion.

It's natural to have a different point of view. It's natural and normal to have a different way of understanding. And it's definitely normal for someone else to disagree with your ways of dealing with things.

Most of us don't want to see someone disagreeing with us because we have this tricky little fellow inside of us that we call EGO.

Our ego makes us feel disappointed when we see or hear someone doing or saying something better than us. We cannot let go of the fact that someone might be right or that someone might be Okay with being wrong and we can't do a single thing about it.

This conflict of values occurs within ourselves as well. We want to do one thing but we cannot leave the other thing as well. We want to have something but we cannot keep it just because we don't have the resources to maintain them.

This feeling of 'want to have but cannot have' makes us susceptible to feelings of incompleteness ultimately making us depressed. The reality of life is that you can't always get what you want. But that doesn't make it a good enough reason to give up on your dreams or stop thinking about other things too.

Life has a lot to offer to us. So what if you can't have this one thing you wanted the most. Maybe it wasn't meant for you in the first place. Nature has a way of giving you blessings even when you feel like you have nothing.

Let's say you want something but your mind tells you that you can't have it. So what you should do is to find alternative ways to go around your original process of achieving that thing and wait for new results. What you should do is to give up on the idea altogether just because you have a conflict within your personality.

You cannot let this conflict that is building within you get a hold of you. Clear your mind, remove all doubts, get rid of all your fears of failure or rejection, and start working from a new angle with a new perspective. Set new goals and new gains from the same thing you wanted the first time. This time you might get it just because you already thought you had nothing to lose.

This feeling of 'No Regret' will eventually help you get over any situation you ever come across after a fight with your inner self. This feeling can help you flourish in any environment no matter what other people say or do behind your back.

Nothing can bring you peace but yourself. Nothing holds you back but your other half within you.

Chapter 28:

8 Things To Do When You Like Someone More Than You Thought You Would

Finding someone in life that can be your companion can be quite a journey. You will meet people who like to play games, who are wild and crazy, and those who are just downright unpleasant to be around. You will go on dates that you just want to quickly get out of and head home. But what happens when you meet someone who just seems like the perfect fit for you. When that person seem to sync with you on every wavelength and frequency. What would you do?

You feel your heart bursting out of your chest. You ask yourself is this real life or is it just fantasy (quote from Bohemian Rhapsody if you got that reference)? You felt like you've never connected with someone so deeply and emotionally before and you are just not sure what to make of these intense feelings.

You talk on the phone for hours without running out of things to say. He or she is able to guess your next sentence as if they were reading your mind. And you feel like you've been searching your whole life for this person. Going through guy after guy, or girl after girl, sifting through the noise, and this golden gem has finally presented itself to you.

In today's topic we will go through XX ways that you can do to move forward. Tips on how you can navigate that path forward and make a relationship that lasts a lifetime.

1. Embrace These Feelings

Having butterflies in your stomach or feeling like your heart is overflowing could be signs that you are fully attracted to this person that you've found in your life. They have got your undivided attention and there is no one else that you are thinking of but him or her. Embrace these feelings. Accept that they are there to point a path to you. That you feel these things for a reason. Don't try to brush them aside or hide it under a mat thinking ignorance is bliss. As humans we are feeling creatures, so take these emotions and use them to your advantage.

2. Don't Rush Things

When we like someone a lot, it can be easy for us to get caught up in the moment. We want to see the person every single day and we obsess over their texts and calls. Stop and take a breather. If you want a long-lasting relationship with this person, take things slow. There is no incentive for you to rush things if you foresee a long future ahead. Resist the urge to expect that the person will reciprocate the same intensity at the beginning phases of your relationship. Instead take it one step at a time. Don't rush into bed. Dating takes time.

3.   Always Be Yourself

It is easy for us to want to present the best front of ourselves when we are trying to woo the other person that we really like. We may change what we say or do to accommodate the other person because we want them to like us. But if we take it too far, we may lose our sense of identity in the process. Always make sure that you stay true to yourself. The other party has to like you for you, and not who you pretend to be. If that person is right for you, he or she will accept you for who you are and all the quirks that you may bring to the table.

4.   Stay Committed To Other Areas of Your Life

Obsessing over someone can become a bad habit for us if we are not mindful of our thoughts and actions. We may have a tendency to prioritise all the time and energy into that person while forgoing all the things we know we should be doing. We lose focus at work, is disinterested in family time, and we may even neglect our friends in the process. Always remember that those are the pillars of your life and to not waver in your commitment to them even though someone new and amazing has entered into your life.

5.   Give The Person Time To Warm Up To You

We may feel strongly for the person, but it doesn't necessarily mean that they feel the exact same way about us right away. Building a relationship takes time, and we need to be mindful that things don't simply blossom overnight. A plant takes constant watering and sunlight to flower, and the same goes for courting and dating. Let the person see who you are gradually. Show them a different page of your book to them over time and let them enjoy you from cover to cover rather than giving them a spark-notes summary.

6. Go On Regular Dates

A good way to mesh your two lives together is to go on regular dates. Express little nuggets of interest to them every time you hang out. That way you are releasing some of that built up feelings you have inside you a little at a time. The last thing you want to do is scare the other person away by being too intense and overwhelming. Spending time together is a good way to also see if you are compatible and a good fit for each another.

7. Find New Things To Do Together

Finding new places to hang out, new things to eat, and new things to do, keeps things fresh between the two of you. That way you get to experience what that person is like in different places and settings. You may pick up more on their likes and dislikes that way. Don't forget to take things slow even though you are trying new things together.

8. Take It To The Next Level

If you feel like you've reached a point where you are certain that you like this person, and that he or she feels the same way about you, it may be time to take things to the next level. However long this process takes, ensure that both of you are on the same page. The last thing you want to do is face a rejection or ask too prematurely. Let things happen naturally, that way there is no second guessing.

Conclusion

Managing your feelings for someone you like a lot can be a tricky thing, but hopefully these tips will help you navigate through it all. I sincerely hope that you are able to build a life-long relationship with this treasured person as well. Life is too short to let good people slip by us.

Chapter 29:

Contribute To Society In A Meaningful Way

Today we are going to talk about how and why you should do work that contributes to society in a meaningful way. And the benefits that it can bring to all aspects of your life, be it psychological, sociological, or physical.

Why do I feel that this topic is of importance that I should highlight it in today's episode? Well because if there is one thing i have noticed about my salaried friend workers around me, I do feel that they lack a bigger vision and purpose for their life. And i feel that there is a sense that the end goal of their work is not to the benefit of their own personal growth, but of the $ sign at the end. And this motivation to work towards a 5 figure pay check is one that ultimately brings not much joy and meaning to one's life.

The many friends that I have interviewed have told me repeatedly that these jobs are merely a means to an end. That it's a routine that they have pretty much resigned themselves to sustain a lifestyle that they feel is good enough for them. This mentality has gotten me to question the culture of whether a monetary goal is truly sufficient in making one truly happy. Yes to an extent, money can bring about freedom which would free up time for one to pursue their passions in life, but for most, this race towards $10k just feels futile.

I would argue that only when you know what to do with freedom of time, and that is to serve a purpose greater than your own selfish needs, can you truly have a meaningful time on this earth.

The greatest entrepreneurs today make their millions not by chasing the money per se, but rather by finding problems that they can solve. They find a gap in society, a need that needs to be filled, and invent a novel solution to a problem that aims to address those holes. Think Jeff Bezos, Steve Jobs, Elon Musk, Mark Zuckerberg. These billionaires have their customers and consumers in mind when they set out to create their mega companies that have largely dominated our world today.

Now I am not saying you need to be doing these crazy big deals to live a happy life, but i believe that everyone has an ability to start somewhere, to start small in our community. If you have no desire for entrepreneurship and are contented with being a salaried worker, that is absolutely perfect. However you can consider doing some volunteer work, and working with a community that can better the lives of someone out there even if it just by a little bit. I guarantee that these selfless acts of giving your time to help someone out in your unique way will reward you with a feeling that money just can't buy.

If you feel like you can do more, you can dedicate more of your time to a particular cause that resonates with you, that you will not feel like a chore to serve. A cause that strikes your heart and soul that makes you want to go back so that you can give more and do more.

Maybe this cause will be something you might end up dedicating your life to, you never know. But I do know that chasing money and dedicating your life to making money will never make you happy. Invest in others, invest in their spirit, invest in doing good for society will be infinitely more worthy of your time and energy.

I challenge you today to see in what areas can you contribute to society and do good for others. I believe that you will not only feel purpose, but it will help sustain you in your career and work as well, giving you a fresh perspective on what life is really all about.

Chapter 30:

6 Steps To Focus On Growth

Growth is a lifelong process. We grow every moment from the day we are born until our eventual death. And the amazing thing about growth is that there is no real limit to it.

Now, what exactly is growth? Well, growing is the process of changing from one state to another and usually, it has to be positive; constructive; better-than-before. Although growth occurs equally towards all directions in the early years of our life, the rate of growth becomes more and more narrowed down to only a few particular aspects of our life as we become old. We become more distinctified as individuals, and due to our individuality, not everyone of us can possibly grow in all directions. With our individual personality, experiences, characteristics, our areas of growth become unique to us. Consequently, our chances of becoming successful in life corresponds to how we identify our areas of growth and beam them on to our activities with precision. Let us explore some ways to identify our key areas of growth and utilize them for the better of our life.

1.   Identify Where You Can Grow

For a human being, growth is relative. One person cannot grow in every possible way because that's how humans are—we simply cannot do every thing at once. One person may grow in one way while another may grow in a completely different way. Areas of growth can be so unlike that one's positive growth might even seem like negative growth to another person's perspective. So, it is essential that we identify the prime areas where we need to grow. This can be done through taking surveys, asking people or critically analyzing oneself. Find out what lackings do you have as a human being, find out what others think that you lack as a human being. Do different things and note down where you are weak but you have to do it anyway. Then, make a list of those areas where you need growing and move on to the next step.

2. Accept That You Need To Grow In Certain Areas

After carefully identifying your lackings, accept these in your conscious and subconscious mind. Repeatedly admit to yourself and others that you lack so and so qualities where you wish to grow with time.

Never feel ashamed of your shortcomings. Embrace them comfortably because you cannot trully change yourself without accepting that you need to change. Growth is a dynamic change that drags you way out of your comfort zone and pushes you into the wild. And to start on this endeavor for growth, you need to have courage. Growth is a choice that requires acceptance and humility.

3. Remind Yourself of Your Shortcomings

You can either write it down and stick it on your fridge or just talk about it in front of people you've just met—this way, you'll constantly keep reminding yourself that you have to grow out of your lackings. And this remembrance will tell you to try—try improving little by little. Try growing.

It is important to remain consciously aware of these at all times because you never know when you might have to face what. All the little and big things you encounter every day are all opportunities of growth. This takes us to the fourth step:

4. Face Your Problems

Whatever you encounter, in any moment or place in your life is an opportunity created: an opportunity for learning. A very old adage goes: "the more we learn, the more we grow". So, if you don't face your problems and run away from them, then you are just losing the opportunity to learn from it, and thus, losing the opportunity of growing from it. Therefore, facing whatever life throws at you also has an important implication on your overall growth. Try to make yourself useful against all odds. Even if you fail at it, you will grow anyway.

5. Cross The Boundary

So, by now you have successfully identified your areas of growth, you have accepted them, you constantly try to remind yourself of them and you face everything that comes up, head on—never running away. You are already making progress. Now comes the step where you push yourself beyond your current status. You go out of what you are already facing and make yourself appear before even more unsettling circumstances.

This is a very difficult process, but if you grow out of here, nothing can stop you ever. And only a few people successfully make it through. You create your own problems, no one might support you and yet still, you try to push forward, make yourself overcome new heights of difficulties and grow like the tallest tree in the forest. You stand out of the crowd. This can only be done in one or two subjects in a lifetime. So make sure that you know where you want to grow. Where you want to invest that much effort, and time, and dedication. Then, give everything to it. Growth is a life's journey.

6. Embrace Your Growth

After you have crossed the boundary, there is no turning back. You have achieved new heights in your life, beyond what you thought you could have ever done. The area—the subject in which you tried to develop yourself, you have made yourself uniquely specialized in that particular area. You have outgrown the others in that field. It is time for you to make yourself habituated with that and embrace it gracefully. The wisdom you've accumulated through growth is invaluable—it has its roots deeply penetrated into your life. The journey that you've gone through while pursuing your growth will now define you. It is who you are.

As I've mentioned in the first line, "growth is a lifelong process". Growth is not a walk in the park, It is you tracking through rough terrains—steep heights and unexplored depths for an entire lifetime. Follow these simple yet difficult steps; grow into the tallest tree and your life will shine upon you like the graceful summer sun.

Chapter 31:

6 Signs You Need To Give Yourself Some Personal Space

While we wish to stay forever in the honeymoon phase of a relationship, we also must keep in mind that it is precisely what we call it; only a phase. Not every relationship is sunshine and rainbows every day. A relationship is between two individuals who both have individual needs. Sometimes, those needs include having some alone time with themselves. But how and when exactly do you know if you need some space from your partner?

April Masini, a New York-based relationship expert and author, says, "If you can't make it an hour or two without checking in or asking a question of your partner, you need a break." Needing space in your relationship does not in any way means that you don't love your partner anymore; it simply means that you need some time to get recharge and take care of yourself. Here are some signs that you need to give yourself some personal space.

1. You Feel Stressed Out

Suppose you're unnecessarily stressed out, even if it isn't coming from your relationship. In that case, it's probably a good idea to spend some alone time and ponder over things. It can be some underlying tension coming from work or family, or it might be something in your relationship that you want but are not necessarily getting it. Taking some time out for yourself and figuring out where your stress is coming from or what's been upsetting you, you will then be better positioned to sort out your problems and discuss those issues with your partner.

2. You Don't Feel Like yourself

A significant sign indicating that you need some alone time for yourself is if you are started to feel exhausted, irritable, or simply just not yourself. Everyone should know the importance of needing some me time for yourselves. Your partner should understand if you need to take care of yourself and your mental health. Needing space from your partner in no way means that your relationship is at stake or if there's anything wrong with it. It simply means that you both need to spend time with yourself to rest, relax, or spend time with other people.

3. You Feel Suffocated

Spending so much time with people can prove fatal and can lead to being co-dependent on them, which is ultimately the kiss of death. It is assumed that, as a couple, you both should naturally be spending all of your time together, but there is such a thing as seeing too much of each other. It is essential to pull away and have some time for yourself. Find a hobby, take a walk, read a book. The more you spend your time with a person, the more likely you will get tired of each other soon. You need to get yourself some personal space not to get suffocated and overwhelmed by your relationships with other people.

4. You Don't Have any Outside Interests

Do you have any interests of your own, or do you rely entirely on the other person and their hobbies? It's healthy to have some things in common with your partner, but not all of them. Suppose you follow and copy their hobbies and interests and don't have any of your own. In that case, it might lead to some adverse psychological effects. Suppose they leave you or are just too busy to see you; you'll be left with nothing but boredom and waiting for the other person to catch up to you again. You need to give yourself space and find out what you like as an individual. Find your hobbies and passions, grow fond of them, and then work on them independently.

5. Spending Time With Them Is Draining You Out

If you aren't having as much fun as you used to have while meeting them, then you should take some space for yourself. If you're feeling drained out and low on energy after every interaction, it's time to spend some time apart. You get frustrated and irritated easily and don't make any efforts to resolve a fight. Patch-ups seem challenging for you; if your interactions are painful and difficult, then consider some alone time to gather your thoughts.

6. Your Vibe's Getting A Bit Off

Although there can be many reasons for this, stress, depression, exhaustion, etc., the primary cause can be that you're not getting enough space to deal with your emotions and feelings. Your relationship feels strained, and you feel like escaping from everything. This is the best time to ask for space from everyone and everything and ponder over whatever's bothering you.

Conclusion

Everyone deserves a relationship with more positivity than negativity in it. It's okay to need some space for yourself now and then. Evaluate your needs and try to figure out what you want.

Chapter 32:

Dealing With Worries

Everyone worries from time to time. Too much worry can be bad as it leaves us feeling tense and anxious. Even though we might say to ourselves and others – "Stop worrying. It's pointless. It won't do any good" – there is something about worrying that makes it hard to stop. This is because worry can be helpful.

Useful worry prompts action. All other worry is pointless.

• Worry is useful if it makes you pay attention

Worrying about the weather cannot stop it raining on your washing; however, if you watch the sky and act to bring in your washing when it rains, being aware that it will have helped.

• Worry is useful, provided it is turned into a plan for action

For example, worrying that your electricity might get cut off might lead you to act to pay your bill on time. Once the bill has been paid, the worrying would stop, and you would feel better.

• Worry is useful if it helps you be better prepared

Worry may help you think about "what you could do if...," or "what would happen if...". Worrying "what would happen if my house was burgled" could make you act to take out house insurance and lock your front door when you go out.

Worry without action does nothing

I worry on its own did something then we could worry all day to increase our bank balance. On the other hand taking action such as selling something, working more hours, or spending less will directly affect our bank balance.

Is it worth worrying about?

Four things are not worth worrying about, but that account for many of our worries: the unimportant, the unlikely, the uncertain, and the uncontrollable. Ban these from your life, and you will worry less.

The Unimportant

It is easy to fill your life with worries about little things. When you find yourself worrying, start to question yourself instead. Ask yourself, "How important is the thing that I am worried about?"

Here are three points to help you answer this question.

1. **The five-year rule**: Ask yourself: "will this matter in 5 years?" This is a way of looking at your worry from a long-term point of view. View your worries differently: will this still be a concern in a week, a month, or a year?

2. **The measuring rod**: Ask yourself: "Where, on a scale of bad experiences, is the thing I'm worried about?" Think about a very

bad experience you have had. How does your current worry feel when compared with this?

3. **The calculator:** Ask yourself: "How much worry is this worth?" We only have a certain amount of time and energy. Make sure you do not spend more worry on your problem than it is worth. You need your time and energy for more important things. Maybe some time you would have spent worrying could be used for doing something.

Chapter 33:

10 Habits of Prophet Muhammad

The Prophet Muhammad (peace be upon him) is a great man believed to have been a prophet of Allah. Born in Mecca about 570 in the common era (570 CE), the man who founded the Islam religion lived for sixty-two years, until he died in 632 CE.

Throughout his life, he was an inspiration to many people who believed in his calling. He lived an exemplary life and his followers emulated his habits. Here are ten habits of the prophet:

1. **He Was A Man Of Unquestionable Integrity**

The prophet led an honest life to the point even his staunchest enemies would vouch for him. Like other prophets in Islam; Ibrahim, Ismail, and Yusuf, prophet Muhammad was a truthful and very noble man.

At one time the prophet (peace be upon him) assembled all the Makkans in one place and asked them if they would believe him when he said that an army was approaching. Everybody said they will trust him because they have never heard him lie. The people believed him completely to trust him with their lives.

2. **He Was Influential**

Everywhere the prophet gave his speech, he managed to influence people to abandon their evil ways and draw closer to God. His speech rattled his enemies and they could not comprehend how he was able to command such a large following because his believers increased daily.

His influence, even in death, has not withered away. The world has at least 1.8 billion Muslims who believe in Islam and the doctrines that the prophet (peace be upon him) advanced.

3. <u>He Was Bold and Courageous</u>

Prophet Muhammad (peace be upon him) spoke fearlessly of God's message. He criticized rich merchants for their immorality and greed as they exploited the poor. He also spoke against ills in society with a call to action to reform.

Even when the prophet faced death threats, he remained firm in his resolve to fight injustice. His focus was to spread the message of Allah to the whole world.

4. <u>He Was Fair</u>

It can never be said that the Prophet (peace be upon him) has never been unfair throughout his documented life. He stood and championed for fairness regardless of who was right or wrong. His sole aim was to live the life of equity he was preaching.

There was once a dispute between a Jewish person who had been framed and a Muslim. He ruled in favor of the Jew after sufficient evidence was put before him. Were it not that he was fair, he could have sided with the Muslim.

5. <u>He Was Apt</u>

The prophet (peace be upon him) was fast and ready prepared for any eventuality. This made him the perfect leader. In him was a reliable person capable of representing them well.

He was an advocate of consulting. In his line of work, he would decide and act almost immediately. There was a time when he was preparing for a military expedition and a companion came to question him on the military plan. The prophet (peace be upon him) knew the different times of discussion and action. He did not allow himself to be distracted during such a crucial time.

6. <u>He Showed Servant Leadership</u>

Prophet Muhammad (peace be upon him) did not lead people to causes he did not believe in. He was at the forefront with his followers following behind. His words were laced with action and you could be sure he would abandon everything to attend to a bigger cause.

The prophet (peace be upon him) once said that the leader of a people is their servant. He did not believe in burdening his followers with his baggage. He served the people.

7. <u>He Was Patient</u>

The prophet (peace be upon him) was very patient to lengths that ordinary people could not attain. His patience was limitless and he did not complain when he passed through painful moments in his life.

In Ta'if, the people and their children stoned him until he was bleeding. He patiently endured the suffering while watching his followers being mistreated. It is his great patience that strengthened his followers to endure trials.

8. <u>He Demonstrated Emotional Maturity</u>

Prophet Muhammad (peace be upon him) was always positive despite prevailing difficult times. He insisted on self-happiness as well as that of other people. Even when it was expected that he would revenge on his enemies, the prophet showed emotional intelligence and forgave them.

The prophet taught that smiling was also a form of charity. This was not the face-value meaning of his statement. He was directing his followers to rise above petty squabbles and work towards positivity and emotional maturity just like him.

9. <u>He Was Compassionate</u>

Prophet Muhammad (peace be upon him) was compassionate to everyone. He did not hold grudges against his enemies. Instead, he would sympathize with their misfortunes and help them overcome them.

He once showed care and compassion by visiting an old woman who tormented him by throwing litter his way. The prophet (peace be upon him) helped her prepare food when she fell sick. He did not remember the ill she had done to him.

10.<u>He Was A Peacemaker</u>

Prophet Muhammad (peace be upon him) did not thrive in chaos and disorderliness. He was a peacemaker and intervened to calm a situation that could have turned chaotic. So understanding was he that he once stopped his followers from beating up a man who urinated in the mosque!

A Bedouin had come to a mosque of the prophet and urinated within the prayer area. The worshippers were angered and wanted to beat up the Bedouin. It is prophet Muhammad (peace be upon him) who intervened and defended the man.

He understood that it was a call of nature and the man could not stop himself. Were it not for the prophet's peace-keeping habit, the Bedouin could not survive the anger of the believers.

In conclusion, these are the ten pillar habits of prophet Muhammad (peace be upon him). They are dominant habits throughout his life.

Printed in the USA
CPSIA information can be obtained
at www.ICGtesting.com
LVHW051134160923
758405LV00044B/962